Acknowledgements

Photos: pp. 2, 6, 22 © Camera Press Ltd, p. 14 © Keystone,
pp. 17, 19, 28 © Hulton Deutsch Collection Ltd, p. 25 © Corbis.
Cover photo: © Popperfoto.

Orders: please contact Bookpoint Ltd, 39 Milton Park, Abingdon, Oxon OX14 4TD. Telephone: (44) 01235 400414, Fax: (44) 01235 400454. Lines are open from 9.00–6.00, Monday to Saturday, with a 24 hour message answering service. Email address: orders@bookpoint.co.uk

British Library Cataloguing in Publication Data
A catalogue record for this title is available from The British Library

ISBN 0 340 72066 2

First published 1994
Impression number 10 9 8 7 6 5 4 3 2 1
Year 2003 2002 2001 2000 1999 1998

Copyright © 1994, 1998 The Basic Skills Agency.

Typeset by Fakenham Photosetting Ltd, Fakenham, Norfolk.
Printed in Great Britain for Hodder & Stoughton Educational, a division of Hodder Headline Plc, 338 Euston Road, London NW1 3BH by Page Bros Ltd, Norwich.

John F. Kennedy

Mike Wilson

Published in association with The Basic Skills Agency

Hodder & Stoughton

A MEMBER OF THE HODDER HEADLINE GROUP

Contents

In May 1962,
Marilyn Monroe went to a birthday party.
The President of the United States,
John Fitzgerald Kennedy,
was 45 years old.

Marilyn stood on stage
in the spot-light.
She wore a see-through dress.
She blew kisses at Kennedy,
and sang in a sexy voice:

'Happy Birthday Mr President,
Happy Birthday to you!'

People began to wonder:

Was the President having an affair
with the Hollywood star?

Three months later, Marilyn was dead.
Some say she was murdered,
because she knew too much.

Next year, President Kennedy was dead too,
shot in the head in Dallas, Texas.

Both of these deaths
were surrounded by gossip and mystery.

For over 30 years,
people have been trying to find out
what is the truth and what is rumour.
Millions of words have been written.
In the White House in America,
there is a huge library,
full of books and papers and photos,
all about President Kennedy's death.

But we may never know all the facts
about the life and death
of John F Kennedy.

1 Young Jack

John F Kennedy was born in Boston,
on 29 May 1917.
(His name was John,
but everyone called him 'Jack'.)
He was one of nine children
in an Irish Catholic family.

The Kennedys were rich.
His father, Joseph Kennedy
was a banker,
a self-made man
who became US Ambassador to Britain
before World War Two.

Joseph pushed his sons hard.
He said that the world was a jungle.
You had to fight and compete
for what you wanted.

Winning was everything.

So Joseph Kennedy taught his children
to fight and compete:
in games, in sports, in everything.
Even the girls, John's sisters,
had to fight just as hard as the boys.

But the family was always very close.
And by 1929, when young Jack was 12,
each of the Kennedy children
was a millionaire.

Their father wanted what was best for them.

He wanted the Kennedys
to dominate American public life.
He wanted one of them
to be the first Catholic
to become President of the United States.

The Kennedy family.

When he was still young,
Jack Kennedy had scarlet fever.
In fact, he was often ill as a child.

His mother tried to feed him up
because he needed it.

'He had a narrow face,
his ears stuck out,
his hair wouldn't stay put.'

He looked like an elf,
a cheeky little elf.
But always full of energy,
always full of charm.

2 War

In World War Two,
John Kennedy's life changed for ever.

He fought in the war,
and almost died.

He was captain of a gun-boat,
called PT 109,
fighting the Japanese
in the Pacific Ocean.

In August 1943,
a Japanese destroyer rammed PT 109,
and cut it in two.
There was a huge explosion,
and part of the boat went down
in a ball of flame.

In fact,
only two of the 13 crew died
in the explosion.
The rest hung on
to what was left of PT 109.

They were lost in Japanese waters,
40 miles behind enemy lines.
There were sharks in the seas
all around them.
They had no food or water.
Some were badly burned.

But they were alive.

Kennedy and his men swam for miles
until they got to land.
A tiny island. 30 metres across.

Kennedy did what he could
to keep their spirits up.
He swam out again,
to try and get help.
But he failed.
He just came back
even more exhausted.

Next day he swam to a bigger island.
He found food and water and sweets
left there by the Japanese.
He took them back to his men.

He also found two local men.
They were working as scouts
for the Americans.

Kennedy wrote a message
inside a coconut shell:

'11 ALIVE
NEED SMALL BOAT
KENNEDY.'

The scouts set off through enemy lines
to take the message to the American base.

In the end, they got through,
and Kennedy and his men were rescued.
They had survived on coconuts and rainwater
for eight days.

Back in America,
John Kennedy was a war-hero.
He won a medal for his bravery.

But he just joked about it.
'I couldn't help it,' he said.
'They sank my boat.'

Kennedy's older brother, Joe Junior,
also fought in the war.
He flew bomber planes
in the US Air Force.

In August 1944,
Joe's plane took off in the south of England.
He was going to bomb France.

After only twenty minutes in the air,
the plane blew up.
Joe was still over England.
Ten tons of TNT exploded,
and scattered bits of the plane
over miles of the countryside below.

Joe was never found.

Four years later,
John's sister, Kathleen
also died in a plane crash.

The father of the Kennedy family,
Joseph Senior,
had pushed his eldest son
to go into public life.
But now Joe Junior was dead.

John Kennedy said later:

'I went into politics
because Joe died.
And if anything happened to me tomorrow,
my brother Bobby would run
for my seat in the Senate.
And if Bobby died,
Teddy would take over for him.'

Jack said these words in the 1950s.
Back then, he could not know
that within ten years,
all of his words would come true.

In 1946,
Jack Kennedy went into politics
as a Democrat.

He stood for higher wages,
lower prices, lower rents,
and more help for the elderly.

He was charming,
a good-looking war-hero.
He knew he had sex appeal.

This appeal grew, in 1953,
when he married Jackie Lee Bouvier,
a rich, well-bred society beauty.

John F Kennedy and his wife, Jackie.

In 1960,
Kennedy won the election for President.

The other candidate was the Republican,
Richard Nixon.

Kennedy won by only a few votes.
Nixon had been favourite.
But the turning point came
in four television debates
between the two men.

Kennedy looked good.
He was calm and clever in the debates.
Nixon looked tired and shifty.
He looked like he needed a shave.

It was the first time
television had been used in an election.
And it was the first time
television helped to decide
the election result.

3 The President

The new President was 43,
the youngest US President ever.

In a few months
he made his first big mistake.

On 17 April 1961
15,000 Cuban exiles
landed in the Bay of Pigs in Cuba.

They had US guns
and were helped by the CIA.
They wanted to bring down Fidel Castro,
the Communist leader in Cuba.

The raid was a flop,
and President Kennedy had to back down.
He sent food and medicine to Cuba
to say sorry.

But the CIA still went on
with secret plans to kill Castro.

Kennedy being sworn in as President of the USA.

Next year, in October 1962,
US planes spotted nuclear missiles
– built by Russia –
right on their doorstep in Cuba.

President Kennedy told the Russians
to remove the rockets.
If they didn't, America would bomb them,
and start a nuclear war.

For 13 days,
the world held its breath.

Then the Russians backed down.
The Cuban Crisis was over.
Kennedy had won
the deadly game of bluff.

After the Cuban Crisis,
President Kennedy had plans
to be more friendly with Russia.

He had plans
to get America out of the war in Vietnam.
And he wanted to give more rights
to black people and poor people
all over America.

But all his plans were cut short
on 22 November 1963,
in Dallas, Texas.

4 Dallas

Kennedy went to Texas
because he had political enemies there,
and he wanted to win them to his side.

At noon a line of cars left the airport
and drove JFK into town.
The President sat in an open car,
waving to the crowds.

In the car with him
were his wife, Jackie Kennedy
and the Governor of Texas,
John Connally and his wife.
There were no security men in the car
to protect the President.

The President's car slowed
as it turned out of Elm Street.

For the next six seconds,
the air was full of rifle fire.

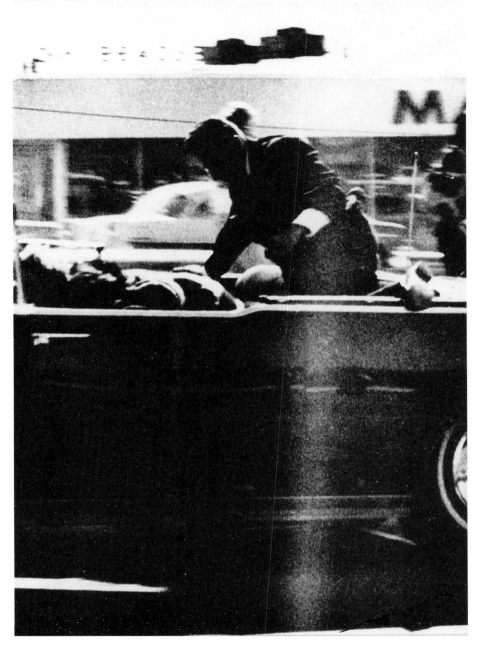

President Kennedy, shot in Dallas, Texas.

The President fell back,
covering his wife with blood.
He had been hit in the neck, the back
and in the side of the head.

The shooting seemed to come
from two places at the same time:
from a building
a long way behind the President's car;
and from some trees just in front.

The President's car raced to hospital,
but JFK could not be saved.

A few hours later,
police arrested Lee Harvey Oswald
for the murder of John F Kennedy.

Oswald was a poor, strange no-hoper.
He was mixed up in crime
and left wing politics.
He was known to the FBI and the CIA.

He was in Dallas
on the day of the murder.
He worked in the building
the rifle shots came from.
But he was a poor shot,
and he could not have fired all the bullets
which hit the President and two other men.

Did Oswald really shoot Kennedy?
Did he work alone or did he have help?
Or was he innocent?
Was he 'set up' by other people?

We will never know Oswald's story.
Two days after his arrest,
he was shot and killed by Jack Ruby,
who worked for the FBI and the CIA.

Jack Ruby died in prison a few years later.

5 That Was the President ...

President John F Kennedy
was still young and handsome
when he died.
And the youngest ever President
became the youngest to die.

He was the best-loved President in America
since Abraham Lincoln
(and Lincoln was *also* shot
and killed, in 1865).

We may never find out
how John F Kennedy was murdered,
or why he had to die.

Now, over 30 years on,
America remembers the President as a hero.

They see his death
as the death of Hope.
They see his murder
as the murder of the American Dream.